STEPPER THE DREAM HORSE

The True Story of a Girl, Her Dream, and Her Horse

by Laurel Swift-Floyd

Illustrations by
Kevin Jones

TEACH Services, Inc.
PUBLISHING
www.TEACHServices.com • (800) 367-1844

World rights reserved. This book or any portion thereof may not be copied or reproduced in any form or manner whatever, except as provided by law, without the written permission of the publisher, except by a reviewer who may quote brief passages in a review.

The author assumes full responsibility for the accuracy of all facts and quotations as cited in this book. The opinions expressed in this book are the author's personal views and interpretations, and do not necessarily reflect those of the publisher.

This book is provided with the understanding that the publisher is not engaged in giving spiritual, legal, medical, or other professional advice. If authoritative advice is needed, the reader should seek the counsel of a competent professional.

_____

Copyright © 2019 Laurel Swift-Floyd
Copyright © 2019 TEACH Services, Inc.
ISBN-13: 978-1-4796-1020-4 (Paperback)
ISBN-13: 978-1-4796-1021-1 (ePub)
Library of Congress Control Number: 2019911405

Original song "Clippity Clop" by Laurel Swift-Floyd
Original cookie recipe by Laurel Swift-Floyd

Published by

www.TEACHServices.com • (800) 367-1844

Table of Contents

Dedication 4

Chapter One: A Dream Come True 5
Chapter Two: Bringing Stepper Home 18
Chapter Three: Saving Laurel's Life 25
Chapter Four: First Place! 34

Epilogue 44

Dedication

To all girls and boys who have a dream.

Chapter One

A Dream Come True

It was June 5th—Laurel's birthday—and she was turning ten. Her mother had made her a beautiful party dress out of lovely periwinkle fabric, which was Laurel's favorite color. It had pretty white ruffles around the neck and arms, with a long white satin sash that wrapped around her waist, tied in a big bow.

She put on her white patent leather shoes and white ruffled socks.

She called to her mother, "Mom, I'm ready."

Her mother combed her long, blond hair, parted it in the middle, and tied it back with blue and white flowers.

She walked into the dining room. The table was decorated with a paper tablecloth that had colorful balloons all over it. There were birthday hats, streamers, blow horns, and a big birthday cake, which had blue, pink, and red roses all around it. The frosting was delicious buttercream with a brown chocolate horse in the middle! Laurel couldn't imagine a more perfect birthday cake.

You see, Laurel loved horses, and every year at Christmas, she and her sister Lily would make cookie ornaments to hang on the tree. Lily would make a ballerina cookie. Laurel would always make a chestnut-brown cookie horse with a blond mane and tail, trying to recreate the horse that she had seen in her dreams.

Last year, on her ninth birthday, her father had gotten her riding lessons at a nearby stable. Laurel loved riding. One day

when she was visiting the stable, she saw a young colt in the arena that looked just like the horse in her dreams. He was galloping so fast, leaving puffs of dust behind him. The wind was blowing through his mane and tail, so
it looked like he was flying.
What a beautiful horse
she thought.

After her riding lesson, she saw Mr. Wright, the stable owner, feeding the horses. She walked over to him and asked, "What is the name of the new horse?"

"His name is 'Robar Master Step,' but we call him 'Stepper.'"

"Can I brush him and give him some treats?"

"Yes, of course you can," replied Mr. Wright.

Laurel, with carrots and apples in hand, walked over to Stepper's stall. As she approached him, he started to neigh.

"Hi, Stepper," Laurel said, and raised her hand to stroke his face. She looked into his beautiful brown, peaceful eyes, and there was an instant bond. This was the horse that she had been dreaming about.

Her father came to pick her up. As he walked towards her, she said, "Daddy, come and see the new horse. His name is 'Stepper.' Isn't he beautiful?"

"He sure is, Honey."

She gave Stepper a big hug and said, "See you next week."

The next few days went by so very slowly! Finally, it was the day her father would take her to the stables for her riding lesson. Most of all, though, she was excited to see Stepper again. When she got there, she went straight to Stepper's stall.

Mr. Wright was standing near the stall, speaking with a lady. Laurel heard him say, "Yes, this is the horse I'm selling."

After the lady left, Laurel asked Mr. Wright, "Why are you selling Stepper?"

Mr. Wright sadly replied, "My tractor broke down, and I need the money to fix it."

Laurel wanted Stepper to be *her* horse, but she knew her dad did not have the money to buy him.

When her dad picked her up, he noticed that she looked so very sad. "What's the matter, Honey?"

"Mr. Wright is selling Stepper. He needs the money to fix his tractor."

"Oh, Honey, I'm so sorry."

Laurel's dad brought her home. Then he went back to the stables to talk to Mr. Wright.

"You know how Laurel loves Stepper, and, if it's possible, I would like to fix your tractor in payment for Stepper." Her dad was an airplane mechanic, and he could fix anything.

Mr. Wright agreed. "Okay, you've got yourself a deal." Then they shook hands.

"Oh, one more thing," her dad said. "We need to keep this a secret from Laurel."

Two days before Laurel's tenth birthday he was finished with the tractor. When Mr. Wright saw the tractor, he could not believe his eyes. That old rusty tractor looked like it was brand new! He gave Laurel's dad the bill of sale, which read, "Robar Master Step, son of Triton Terry and Dolly Physie, a Morgan."

Finally it was 12 o'clock and time for Laurel's friends to arrive and celebrate her birthday. She greeted her friends at the door, and her mother put the birthday presents in the family room around the fireplace.

First "Chuck the Clown" came and did a magic show. He made all kinds of colorful animal balloons and gave one to each of her friends. Then her mother lit the candles on the birthday cake.

"Okay, everybody, gather around the table," she said and the children sang "Happy Birthday." "Laurel," said her mother, "Close your eyes and make a wish."

"I wish, I wish, maybe someday that Stepper could be my horse." Laurel blew out the candles and her mother cut the cake. "Umm! Red velvet! My favorite!"

After they ate the cake, it was time to open the birthday presents. One by one, she opened them all, thanking her friends for their thoughtful gifts. When she was all through, her dad said, "There is one more present you haven't opened yet."

He took her by the hand and walked her to the front door and opened it. Laurel looked across the front lawn, and she could see a horse trailer. A moment later Stepper's head poked out of the back. She looked up questioningly at her dad.

"Go ahead, Honey, he's yours."

She let go of his hand and ran towards the horse trailer with her dad running behind her. She flung open the trailer door and let Stepper out. He had a big periwinkle bow around his neck. She put her hands around his face. "Stepper, you're mine! You're really mine!" Laurel then turned to her father and hugged him. "Thank you, Daddy! Thank you!"

Her wish had come true and so did her dream … and that was the beginning of many adventures that Laurel and Stepper would have for many years to come.

Chapter Two

Bringing Stepper Home

California in September is still hot. It was Sunday and Laurel woke up at 8:00 a.m. She turned to her side and saw her calico cat, "Mimi," snuggled next to her. She patted her head and pinched her little black, fuzzy nose.

Laurel got out of bed and opened her closet door. Her periwinkle dress caught her eye. That's what she was going to wear today because for lunch they were going to go eat at a very special Italian restaurant.

She went into the kitchen and called, "Good morning, Mom and Dad." Her Mom was cooking a nice, hot breakfast for her dad, but Laurel was only going to have just a small bowl of cereal. She wanted to save room for all of the wonderful food at her favorite Italian restaurant, Sorella Restaurant. ("Sorella" means "sister" in Italian.)

Laurel loved the fettuccine alfredo with crispy chicken and broccoli. "Umm, it's so cheesy and creamy."

After lunch they went home and she changed into her English riding outfit. Her dad then took her to the stables where Bonnie, her trainer, gave her riding lessons.

Bonnie had set up the jumps in the arena. She then walked over to Stepper's stall and saw that he was lying down. She could see that he was in a lot of pain. Bonnie knew that if Stepper laid down too long without getting up, the weight of his body would crush his insides, and he would die. Bonnie called Laurel's dad to tell him to come to the stable right away. "Stepper is down and can't get up!"

"Okay, we'll be right there." Her dad called the veterinarian to meet them at the stables. When they arrived, Laurel ran to Stepper's stall. She kneeled down next to his head and softly stroked his face. She was crying, "You have to get up, Stepper! You have to get up!"

He looked at her and moaned. Very soon the veterinarian arrived and immediately took out his stethoscope to listen to Stepper's belly. What he heard was something called "sand colic," which comes from horses eating sand while grazing or eating hay that has been on the ground. The veterinarian pulled on Stepper's halter, and finally got him on his feet. Then he gave him medicine for the colic. After a couple of days, Stepper was feeling much better.

Thankful to have her horse well again, Laurel happily led him out into the arena, galloping around and leaving puffs of dust behind him. He looked amazing, just like the first time she saw him.

For a moment she closed her eyes and imagined living in a beautiful place with lots of land. If only she could! Then she could bring Stepper home!

September fell into October and it was a week before Halloween. Laurel's mom and dad took her out to the country so she could pick out a pumpkin to carve into a jack-o'-lantern. As they were driving along, her dad turned onto a side road. There were trees from side to side. Laurel looked out through the car window and could see the leaves had turned colors: bright red, yellow, and gold, and the sun peeked through them all—it looked like they were lit up.

Further ahead she saw a fast-moving river and mountains all around. Then her dad stopped in front of a little country house with a pumpkin patch and an apple cider stand beside it. Across from the house there was a big, gray barn.

They got out of the car. Her dad went to talk to the property owner, and Laurel and her mom went into the pumpkin patch. Laurel looked around—there were so many pumpkins to choose from! There were big ones, little ones, different colored ones, and bumpy ones. Finally, she found two perfect pumpkins. One she was going to carve into a jumping horse and the other a smiley face. Her mother picked out a small one to make pumpkin pie.

They walked over to the apple cider stand where her dad was still talking to the property owner. Then the owner gave them a glass of apple cider to drink. It was so good, cold, crispy, sweet, and bubbly. They paid for the pumpkins and bought a big jug of apple cider to take home.

On the way back home her Dad asked Laurel, "How did you like that place?"

"I liked it, Daddy; it's such a pretty place."

"Well, do you think Stepper would like it there?"

"Oh, yes, he would love it there!"

"It was for sale, and now it belongs to us."

"Really, Daddy, really!?"

Laurel was so excited. This was the place she had imagined!

"Finally, I can bring Stepper home."

Chapter Three

Saving Laurel's Life

It was a beautiful spring morning. Already four months had passed since Laurel and her family had moved to the country. She loved living there. At the foot of her bed Mimi—her cat—snuggled with a new puppy … a nine-week-old black Labrador Retriever. He was the smallest of the litter, so Laurel called him "Little Guy." He was so adorable. She picked him up and gave him a bunch of kisses.

"When you get older, you can come with me and Stepper on trail rides."

From her bedroom window she could see the red barn with white trim that her dad had painted a couple of days ago. Next to it the green grass mixed in with the bright blue wild flowers—it looked like a field of blue, and she could see Stepper, her beloved horse, his head peeking through the stall door.

He was such a beautiful horse, with his chestnut-brown fur and blond mane and tail. Because Laurel's hair was long and blond, when she bent over to clean his hooves, his head touching hers, you could not tell if the hair was Laurel's or Stepper's.

She put on her blue jeans, boots, red-checkered shirt, and combed her hair into a pony tail. Then she went into the kitchen to have breakfast. Her mother had made pancakes, and Laurel smothered them with fresh raspberry syrup.

"Umm, umm. These are so good!"

As soon as she finished eating, Laurel asked her Mom, "Could we make Stepper's favorite snack—oatmeal and molasses cookies?"

"Ok, Laurel, we can do that. Can you please get the measuring cups out of the cupboard?"

Oatmeal and Molasses Cookies

Recipe:

- 1/2 cup Oatmeal
- 1/2 cup Rolled Oats
- 1 cup Shredded Carrots
- 1 Tbs. Salt
- 1 Tbs. Brown Sugar
- 1/4 cup Water
- 1/4 cup Molasses

Combine all these ingredients in a bowl with non-stick spray. Spray pan, roll into balls, bake for 15 minutes in a 350-degree oven.

After the cookies were baked, Laurel put them on a rack to cool.

It was a perfect day for a trail ride. The cookies would be ready to eat when she got back.

"See you later, Mom. Love you."

Off she went with carrots and apples in hand. However, she had one quick stop to make—she wanted to see the baby chicks that had hatched a couple weeks ago. Both were yellow, but one had black stripes. "Oh, you guys are so, so cute!"

Then she heard Stepper neighing. "Okay, Stepper, I'm coming. I'll be right there."

After Laurel told Stepper good morning, she brushed his forelock away from his face and fed him the carrots and apples. Once he was finished with his treats, Laurel put his bridle on him and climbed on him bareback.

As they galloped down the trail, all of a sudden a big silver-blue crane appeared, flying beside them. Laurel looked at the magnificent bird up in the air. Its body was stretched underneath the large wings; it looked like it was gliding. He followed them for a while and then flew away.

Moving along, they passed an almond orchard that was in bloom. The pretty white flowers were falling gently to the ground and looked like snow.

She also saw squirrels running around, beautiful butterflies flitting, and birds chirping in the trees. Finally, they came to the river. There was the beaver she had seen a couple of days ago. He looked up at her as he was carrying a big branch in his mouth. He slapped his tail on the water and continued building his home. Laurel had named him "George." So, here he was again, carrying mud underneath his chin and putting it in between the leaves and twigs to secure his home. He was almost finished. "I guess that's why they call them 'busy beavers.'" Then she said, "Bye, George! We will see you again soon!"

They were trotting along with a clippity clop. It made Laurel want to sing as the grass turned into rocks, the rocks turned into sand, and the sand turned into water.

"Clippity Clop"

Clippity Clop
Down goes the horse's shoes.
Bang! Boom! Hitting the rocks.
Down goes the rocks, too.
Clippity Clop
Clippity Clop
Down goes the grass from the land
—only sand, water, too.
Clippity Clop
Clippity Clop.

By now she knew Stepper was thirsty. He loved to drink the river water. As they approached a sandy area near the river, all of a sudden the sand turned into quick-sand!

Stepper's front legs were sinking in. As he bent forward to pull himself out, Laurel flew over his head and landed in the quicksand. She was sinking deeper and deeper, still holding onto the reins She looked up at Stepper's face with fear in her eyes.

Stepper knew he had to get her out—NOW! With one big jolt he pulled himself out, Laurel still holding on to the reins. Her feet came out of her boots as Stepper carefully pulled her to safety. She looked back and saw her boots sinking inching down into the quicksand.

She turned her head to Stepper, "Good boy, Stepper. You just saved my life. Good boy!"

Barefoot, Laurel climbed up on a big rock and got on Stepper's back. Slowly, they trotted home.

As they were getting closer to the barn, Stepper started to neigh—he was happy

that they were back home again. Laurel washed him down with a water hose and put him in his stall.

When she went into the tack room to put away her bridle she saw the basket filled with the oatmeal and molasses cookies that she and her mother had made that morning. Laurel brought the basket of cookies to feed Stepper, and of course gave him extras of his favorite oatmeal and molasses treats for saving her life.

Chapter Four

First Place!

Laurel and Stepper had been working hard all year to reach this level.

This was the last horse show of the year, and winning First Place also meant winning the $1,000 prize and the Silver Belt Buckle.

Last year at the same horse show she saw the belt buckle through a glass case. It had a jumping horse on it, and the silver etching around it sparkled like diamonds. It was so beautiful!

The $1,000 prize she wanted to donate to a horse-rescue organization, but most of all she wanted to prove that her horse was a champion and make her family proud.

The day before the horse show, Laurel went to the barn to get Stepper. He was in a playful mood. Stepper's favorite game was playing tag. She walked him into the arena and tagged him. Then he ran off, spinning around, jumping in the air, and running back to tag *her* with *his* muzzle.

When playtime was over, Stepper was ready to be groomed. She washed him and brushed him. Her hand slid across his withers. He felt so soft and silky and he looked great! She put him in his stall and lightly covered him with a sheet to keep him clean for the night. Then she gave him his favorite oatmeal and molasses cookies.

"Get a good night's sleep, Stepper, because tomorrow is going to be a big day," she said as she hugged him good night.

The morning of the horse show, Laurel got up at 5:00 a.m., washed her face, and combed her hair into a ponytail. Then she took out her English riding outfit. The black velvet hat and jacket looked good, but the boots needed polishing. After taking care of that she got dressed.

By now it was 6:00 a.m. The phone rang. Laurel answered it. Her sister Lily was calling to wish her good luck. She was away at college and could not make it for the horse show.

"Thank you, Lilly. I love you! Bye."

After her call with Lilly, Laurel walked over to the barn. As she entered she saw her beloved horse. "Good morning, Stepper."

She took him out of the stall and brushed him. By that time, Bonnie, her trainer, had arrived with the horse trailer. Laurel walked Stepper into the trailer, and then Bonnie shut the door behind him.

Laurel ran back to the house where her mother and father were waiting for her in the car. She opened the rear door, jumped in, put on her seat belt, and off they went. They followed closely behind the horse trailer through winding, mountain roads. All of a sudden, the horse trailer door flew open!

"OH, NO!" everyone gasped.

Laurel's heart was pounding so fast. Her dad was honking the horn to get Bonnie's attention. Bonnie then looked back and saw the open door. She slowly pulled to the side of the road, and Laurel ran towards the trailer.

Stepper's legs were trembling. He turned his head to look at Laurel. He was hanging on for dear life. One false move and he would have fallen out. Bonnie shut the door once again and secured it.

Slowly they drove the rest of the way to the horse show. They finally arrived, a bit shaken. There was no time to ponder what could have happened. Laurel had to concentrate on the horse show.

Her parents went to the stands to watch the show while Bonnie stayed with Stepper. Laurel went to register for the Hunter-Jumper Class and received her competition number. Her number was 47.

Through the loud speaker she heard: "Laurel Swift on Robar Master Step." She rode him into the arena. She looked up into the stands and saw people laughing. You see, Stepper is a *Morgan* horse. His breed is short and stocky, and from the stands he looked more like a pony. Most of the horses that compete are Thoroughbreds. They are a lot taller and bigger, just right for the Hunter-Jumper competition.

It was now time to compete. He galloped to the first jump, lifted his legs high, and easily glided over the poles—"PERFECT." She held him back to the second jump … again, "PERFECT." Third, fourth—people in the stands were cheering. Fifth, Sixth, Seventh … finally the last jump.

Laurel held onto Stepper's reins. She could feel what he was feeling—excited. "NOW, STEPPER!—JUMP NOW!"

PERFECT!

Then came the announcement from the loud speaker: "In first place and the winner of this competition is: Number 47—Laurel Swift on Robar Master Step."

Laurel leaned over Stepper with her
hand on the side of his neck,
and whispered to him,
"We did it, Stepper.
We did it!"

Epilogue

Laurel and Stepper went on to win many more first place competitions and had many more adventures together. On January 29, 2016, Stepper passed away. He was thirty-three. On that day the sun was shining and the rays from the sun surrounded him like shards of crystals and a glowing rainbow appeared across his face.

"My beloved Stepper you will be forever in my heart and I know someday we will ride again."

www.TEACHServices.com • (800) 367-1844

We invite you to view the complete
selection of titles we publish at:
www.TEACHServices.com

We encourage you to write us
with your thoughts about this,
or any other book we publish at:
info@TEACHServices.com

TEACH Services' titles may be purchased in
bulk quantities for educational, fund-raising,
business, or promotional use.
bulksales@TEACHServices.com

Finally, if you are interested in seeing
your own book in print, please contact us at:
publishing@TEACHServices.com

We are happy to review your manuscript at no charge.